DISCOVERING THE POWER
WITHIN YOU

By

Joe Love

PREFACE

We are divine beings, therefore, we have access to the Infinite mind - all knowledge and wisdom is available to us at any point. Consequently, we have unlimited power within us to access this wisdom. Furthermore, there is abundance in the universe and enough for all humanity and god's creations. However, we see that there is inequality and uneven distribution of wealth and resources around us. This is largely because of the ego based fear of some to accumulate, collect, and hoard.

There is an imbalance in the distribution of the resources on this planet; on average, twenty percent of the world's population consumes more than 80 percent of the earth's resources. Indian activist and leader of the Indian independence movement against British rule, Mahatma Gandhi once stated, "The world holds enough to satisfy everyone's needs but not everyone's greed." In these few words, he recognized the main cause of most of the world's social and economic problems. According to World Hunger statistics, there were 795 million people across the world living in poverty in 2017, up from 780 million the previous year.

We are living in the wealthiest and most abundant time in the history of the world. Why do we have hundreds of millions of people in the world starving and living in poverty?

Government is never going to solve this problem. You cannot legislate or pass laws to bring about equality because it is a consciousness problem. If you want prosperity, you have to be coming from a prosperity consciousness. If you are looking for love, then you must be coming from a love consciousness. Your level of consciousness determines where you are in life.

You simply cannot achieve an intention unless you are already at that level of consciousness. The solution lies in spirituality, something that has been in existence before mankind itself. People must change their attitudes and learn to raise their own level of consciousness while at the same time inspiring others to do the same. You do this by living within the spiritual principles of forgiving, sharing, loving, and giving. The problem is we are always looking for a government solution; however, the solution will only be achieved by love and forgiveness. Any strategies that ignore this simple truth waste our time, squander our resources, and undermine our efforts to make a better world.

We are all spirit having a human experience. Man is the only creature endowed with the capacity to separate himself from his body, the senses, emotions, and the mind. He is the user, owner, and master of all these entities. When the intellect is controlling your life, one has no lasting joy; when the ego is the master, one could be dragged into the quagmire. The demands of life require you to use your intuition and discern, "Will this thought, word, or action be in keeping with my highest good?"

In writing this book, it is my hope to show that you have the power to change yourself. When you change the way you think and raise your own level of consciousness, you then have the power to raise the level of consciousness of those around you. If you are unhappy about your present reality, release the old patterns of thinking that have created this present reality. It is your past thoughts that have created your present, and your present thoughts will create your future.

TABLE OF CONTENT

CHAPTER 1

Discover the Power in You

We are born with a link to the Great Spirit of the Universe; the one and only God. This link is something that is constantly at risk of being severed as the forces of the world take hold. Religion is first among the most dangerous of these forces, and its leaders declare that it is original sin and must be wiped out. If people show independence due to a continuation of listening to the voice within, they are targeted and victimised often with ridicule.

This makes people shy to admit that they are linked to the Spirit unless they are in a group of like-minded people. They are the ones who are pouring out of traditional religions and joining the New Age meetings where miracles are happening, and they find peace beyond understanding.

If one is disconnected and looking to re-establish their commitment to their Spirit, it is easy to do.

Following my incarnation, coupled with a strong link to Spirit, I found, my mission to help people discover how to awaken their natural wisdom and find solid footing on a path to spiritual success. I knew my purpose was to assist people in moving through the troubled waters of the mind and into the sanctuary of their spirit.

We are in the time of the end of the day, and everyone who has lived is back in their bodies at this time (Isaiah 26:19). The ones the Spirit is interested in are called the Children of Israel and they are also God's vineyard (Isaiah 5:4, 8). They were seeded with Spirit at the start of the day and have been nurtured until now. They have also suffered and died many times (Job 5:19-22).

The test has been to see who among them will be productive and would have increased in power by now. Who has the strength to reconnect to the real God and come away from the false images that have corrupted the world?

All one has to do to reconnect is to seek the truth with all one's heart, ask for directions, and it will respond.

Be conscious of your thoughts at every integrated moment of existence. In order to awaken the God-mind within you, you must first understand and become conscious of your connection to the Great Universal Spirit.

You are all God and all God is expressed as you; the God-man or God-woman. Read it again and think about this for a minute. Allow this statement to be absorbed into your subconscious mind. "I am all God and all God is expressed as me."

You are made in the image and likeness of God. You are spirit just as God is Spirit, and you have taken on physical form and are able to create just as God. You have the God-ability and the God-power.

Now, let's go further. God is Spirit and the Great Universal Spirit takes on different physical forms or expressions. All that you see is all God and all God is expressed in different physical forms, all being governed by the Divine Intelligence of the Great Universal Spirit.

Let's use a practical example to explain this; an apple tree is made up of all the leaves, branches, trunk, roots, fruit etc., all different physical parts, but all are considered the parts that make up the whole the apple tree. You don't refer to the leaves as the apple tree. It's part of the whole and has its specific function. You don't look at the bark and call it the apple tree. It's all part of the whole and also has its specific function, although we do refer to all the leaves and bark etc. as the apple tree.

Another example would be your body; it's not just your arm or your leg or your face. All parts are different and have different functions, but each part makes up the whole body which is you.

The same thing is true with the Spirit; you are God expressed in physical form. Each part needs the other to fully carry out the whole purpose, the whole divine plan.

Once you become conscious of who you are as part of the divine plan, then your divinity begins the God-mind awakening. As with our apple tree example, the apple tree does not live to itself alone. Its existence works in harmony with everything else around it, drawing life-energy from the sun, the rain, the soil, and wind. Thereby sustaining and providing food, shelter, and nutrients for other people, animals, insects, and even giving back to the soil.

What does this knowledge mean to you? How can it change the way you see yourself?

There are twelve great natural powers or energies within each of us. Each power has a potential to be demonstrated in our personality, comprehended and used by our soul, or exists to motivate us in our lives. These twelve powers are available for our use and expression. We all possess the key to access them. They are available to us all because of the magical gift of free choice.

Due to our differing stages as individual souls growing in understanding and in life experience, it will seem as if one reflects a special talent beyond the capabilities of others, we tend to call such a person gifted or talented as if they are favoured above the rest.

It may seem that is the case, but in the grand scheme of our soul journey, it is rather that they have sought to develop and express one or another of the twelve powers to an extraordinary extent and have perhaps been willing to make this selection and to sacrifice others along the way. We can only applaud others' skills and achievements and should do so generously without any feeling that a particular person is favoured above the rest as we all earn and deserve our fortune, good and bad, from past incarnations and past experiences.

It is best to take a long view and consider that reincarnation is a certainty as is our future life. It is then easier to believe that we have time enough to understand these twelve great powers and on a human level, to use them creatively.

The twelve powers are given different names by different peoples and cultures but in reference to astrology, they are identified as the zodiacal signs that are so familiar; Aries, Taurus, Gemini, Cancer, Leo, Virgo, Libra, Scorpio, Sagittarius, Capricorn, Aquarius and Pisces. Their symbols too, are well known.

When we are born under Aries, when the Sun was in that part of the heavens between the 21st March and the 20th April, the power of self will, adventure, courage, and inner determination is the focus. It may be strongly evident, or yet latent and neglected, awaiting cultivation, depending upon our spiritual nature. But so also are all the other powers that will be called upon throughout our life. It is important to understand that because we happen to be born Aries, in this case, it is only a temporary domination, or perhaps marking a particular responsibility in using this one of the twelve powers. Perhaps we have the power highly developed in order to fulfil our life purpose through bravery of some kind or have a role that requires us to initiate new things. Who knows?

So, because you may be born under one Sun sign does not mean an exclusion of all others, it is just identifying a power of major importance to you in the unique and complex mix that makes up your entire character. All other powers or qualities must also be accessed. To what degree of expression, no one else can measure or judge.

Remember that no one is favoured. We all have the twelve powers available to us. We all have free will that allows us to choose which ones and in what way we wish to draw upon them as we attempt to live our life creatively according to our aspirations and our destiny.

Who are you? I'm not asking about your family or career - what you do or who you're related to. I'm asking if you recognize the power of YOU, the awesome importance God places on and in you. He wants you well, whole, and able to be a *light in the darkness.* You can't do that from a position of sickness or lack. You can't do that if you believe the lie that "I'm not really anybody special." God put you here in this time and place because you are VERY special to Him. He needs you to be healthy and able to be a living epistle, an example of His love, mercy, and grace on the earth.

Your physical health is one-third of your power. It is essential to living the full life God has planned for you. Your mental health is equally important. Most important, however, is your spiritual health. Many of us have been on 'spiritual diets' to the point of emaciation. Sunday lunch (church) isn't enough to feed your spirit all week.

You are special, unique. Like a snowflake, there is no one quite like you! No one on earth has the same exact physical, mental, or emotional appearance that you have. God created you that way.

It was God's grand idea to give His planet to His children - people who were like Him. He planned an inheritance for us - an overflow of bounty and blessing, health and prosperity. Just like an expectant father, He designed this world especially for us. He placed us here to have dominion (Gen. 1:26).

You are here for a reason.

Have you ever put together a jigsaw puzzle... and discovered at the end that there were a few pieces missing? It's a bummer, isn't it? Well, YOU are one of the essential pieces of Life's puzzle. God designed us all to fit together, to complement each other in service to mankind.

If you die early or suffer from mental or physical ailments that prevent you from fulfilling your calling, a piece of our human puzzle is missing. You may seem insignificant to yourself, but it's not true. The world needs each of us - all of us.

The three parts of you are designed to work together for your good - and the good of those around you. That means your spirit is as much a part of your health plan as diet or exercise. Actually, it is the most important part because it is connected to the wisdom and power of God.

He knows how you are put together, why you are the way you are, and what your hot buttons are that trigger overeating, lethargy, depression, and a myriad of other physical challenges. He also knows how to overcome those issues - if you are willing to open your spirit and mind to change.

You have power and great favour!

God put you and me here in this time and place for a reason. You are here to show the world (and share with the people around you) His Love, His Blessing, and His Power. We are to imitate the Father and His Divine Son, Jesus by demonstrating faith and love, patience and self-control. We are to prove God's power through our dominion by overcoming life's challenges including health issues, weight control or bad habits of any kind. You are His example for the world.

The decisions you make, the choices you pick, and the words you speak should reflect, as much as possible, the divine power within you. You are supposed to imitate Jesus, be like the Father, and show the world God's Love and the dominion He gave you.

Over-eating (or any other excess) is a symptom - a compensation for some lack you feel or sense. Excess wrongly tries to fill a spiritual void with physical or emotional things. But God has already provided everything for you that you need. As you develop a deeper relationship with Him, you will discover the power He placed within you to meet every challenge and overcome the tendencies that plague your physical existence.

Lay claim to your divine place in God's family. You are His favourite child. After all, He gave up Jesus to get you! Of course, in His grand plan, He got Jesus back as well, but He wanted you so badly that He was willing to send Jesus from Heaven to make sure you could find your way to Him. Jesus is your big brother. His eternal job is to help you, support all that you do to extend Heaven's reach, and to be your advocate and defender. He's given you all of His power, might, and dominion, and told you to go do what He did.

Created in His Image

God created you in His own image and blessed you with the power to *be fruitful, multiply, replenish, and have dominion.* You can't do that if your physical, mental, or spiritual health is weak or lacking. I challenge you to take a look at your life and lifestyle. Are you becoming all that God wants you to be? He never expects perfection, but He does want you to work toward maturity - the ability and desire to make better choices for your life.

Meditate (dwell on, think about) how awesome it is that God loves you. He has a good plan for you and it includes divine health and blessing. Lay claim to it in your mind until it settles in your spirit as Truth. Until you really believe that God is not only willing, but eager, to help you, you will not experience His power and dominion in your life. Faith believes, without faith it is impossible to please Him. (Heb. 11:6) No matter what challenge you are facing, take a stand of faith that you can overcome it with His grace to help in a time of need (Heb. 4:16)

Who are you? You are the eternal child of God's own heart, chosen by Him to be right where you are, empowered to fulfil His plan for your life. You are special!

CHAPTER 2

Why Love is the Greatest Power in the Universe

Your heart is the most powerful organ in the body.
The hearts controls your feelings of compassion, forgiveness, understanding, generosity, empathy, caring, and of course, love. The heart is the domain of human intimacy. It activates affection, warmth, nurturing friendship and familiarity. On an energy level, it connects the lower ego, your physical self, to the higher soul or spiritual self. The heart is simply the focal point of your spiritual anatomy.

The heart is the most vital organ in the human body as well as our spiritual anatomy. This is because love is the greatest power in the universe. It allows us to channel life's force throughout our whole body

Love is what we all crave the most. It is what we can give the most to make a difference in the world. The heart is the seed of our soul. It is our divine and spiritual essence.

When we open our heart, we begin to connect with our fellow human beings. It is in our heart that we are endowed with the capacity to feel joy, unity, laugh with full bliss, and feel love. It is in the heart that we bring to share the kinds of blessings that we are experiencing with those around us.

An open heart stimulates and activates our highest aspirations, our highest ideals. It brings out the best in us. Our heart brings out the capacity to touch one another in a healing and profoundly sacred way.

When your heart is open, it catapults you into the greatest spiritual potential you have. You begin to realize that you have the potential not only to have an ordinary life, but rather a truly extraordinary, magical, and miraculous life.

The power of love takes you beyond your mortal self and reminds you of who you are; a magnificent spiritual being. When you move into the power of love, you move into the power of miracles. You step into the power of healing and manifestation.

You step into the power of attraction and light-bearing on the planet.

The heart is the gateway to your magnificence, your heritage, and all the blessings the universe has in store for you.

When our heart is open, we feel a sense of flow; we feel valued, uplifted, and nurtured in the deepest sense. We move into our capacity to bring that kind of energy into the world with no strings attached. It activates our ability to begin to contribute to the world instead of just taking.

On the emotional plane, an open heart is the domain of understanding, empathy, and concern for others. Being the centre of love energy from the heart affects our family, children, closest friends, and even our relationships with our pets.

When our heart is open, we care about the effect we have on others. We want to touch others in a positive and nurturing way. We want to bring about healing; we want to help others feel good about themselves.

An open heart helps us shift the energy away from a "me against the world" point of view and begins to put into place a "me as a part of the world" perspective. We can therefore gain the understanding that we are all in this together and we can all be in this together comfortably, happily, and peacefully.

After all, it's being in it together that makes life work. It's the sharing and connectedness that makes your life feels meaningful. You feel that there is no separation between you and other people. When your heart is open, we are all connected and moving towards the same greater good. You realize that every one of us is important and matters equally in the makeup of the universe.

When we think of love, we think of a feeling or an emotion. It takes an action or a movement on our part to express love, and in this sense, love is the greatest power in the universe.

Science and the chakras prove all these activities that go on in the human body once the power of love hits us and causes our heart to open. Science has proven that the heart is the most powerful organ in the human body. The heart charka is the most powerful of all the chakras. What I would like to focus on is the very power of love itself. To fully understand the power of the heart, we have to understand that there is the other side of love. As much as love can bring change and pleasure to those who use it wisely, putting it into the hands of someone who is selfish and looking to always get the upper hand in everything can cause a very destructive force that will destroy lives and damage hearts forever.

Take our same couple who met on that one random meeting. They fall in love and get married and their lives can only ride the waves of feelings and emotion for so long. You see, feelings and emotions go up and down all the time. If I rely on them, I will always be in love one day and out of love the other.

Love is a delicate flower that has to be cared for and nurtured. It cannot be something that you feel and catch and then put it in a cage, and once in a while you throw in some crumbs to feed it. If you do that, I can assure you, love will die. The same thing that brought you into love has to continue for it to survive.

We will change as we grow older and we are changing as individuals all the time. Every romance will change over time because people change. You have to help each other grow and nurture soul growth.

Whatever you give your time to is what you love the most in your life. The guy that spends all his money and time on the golf course is in love with golf. If he is not including his wife in this hobby of his, or indulging in one of hers also, I guarantee you; golf will split them and tear them apart. They may stay together and go through the motions, but the love that sparked all this to happen in the beginning will be gone.

Be individuals but be a couple also. Grow together, not apart. What you did when you couldn't get her out of your mind all those times, continue to do now. I have a friend that is doing everything the right way. He and his wife still go out on dates. He still buys her flowers for no reason. They share things together. They don't let kids and grandkids or work or hobbies keep them apart. Keep things in their proper perspective.

There is a thing that God put into your hearts or it may be that He's just started it with you. Keep it alive. That one circle began with you two. Don't let anyone or anything come into that circle. God made it for you two only. There are other circles that include your children and external family. They are very important also, but the one that started it all, you and her, is exclusive territory. No one can come in unless they have special permission.

Love is usually understood as a strong affection for another, as a strong regard for, and dedication to, someone. It could be for our spouse, our family, our friends...

Love can also be seen as a form of energy. We already know that everything in the Universe is energy in motion. Even the most solid objects are built out of energy. We are surrounded by energy. We ourselves are energy. The source of this energy is love. Love is the highest form of energy.

Energy vibrates at different frequencies. Love forces vibrate at high frequency. Forces of inferior kind show lower frequencies. Love has been seen as the greatest energy of life or the unified field of consciousness.

Those who are in love vibrate at high frequency and can get that frequency throughout the mind and emotions just by recalling the feeling of being in pleasant situations with the beloved ones.

The lack of love opens the door to inferior beings that enter with arms charged with negativity, anxiety, fear, sadness, hate, phobia, etc. Love nourishes health. Negative emotions nourish illness.

Science has shown us that love can heal the body. On the other hand, it has been proven how the absence of love can cause illness and even premature death. The healing love is not really our love. The healing love is God's unlimited love. We are channels that conduct God's love energy for helping in healing. Our love energy is unlimited.

For example, holistic healing professionals send the healing power of love energy from the Universe through their hands and into diseased organs of a sick person's bodies. This healing energy gives the body a tremendous boost to begin the healing process. We do not help others by identifying with their pain. We do help them by channelling the extra Love energy needed to move them beyond their pain.

Today, when every day is a nightmare for many people, when the depression treatments are in such great demand, it is good to remember that love energy generates feelings of joy and happiness in both the receiver and the giver. It produces a flow of physical energy that feeds not only the physical body but the entire being. When you smile and people smile back, love energy has been given out and returned.

If we continuously hold only love in our hearts, we will notice whatever is not in alignment with harmony. We may have to deal with our suppressed remorse, resentment, fear or attachment. We need to clean our subconscious. We have to release all the low frequency energy. With patience and through the regular practice of meditation, we can accomplish this important task.

Prosperity is dependent on having more love in our life. We have to love ourselves unconditionally first before we can truly love someone else. Fear is a big problem for most of us because it blocks higher energy levels and limits our reserves of love.

As said before, love is the most powerful healing energy and it flows by touching others. Our inability to love ourselves, or to give and receive love from others, is the cause of all illnesses. Love is the best natural cure.

CHAPTER 3

Are You Cutting Yourself off from the flow of Love

Most people that I have encountered insist that they have an open, loving, and balanced heart, but from their comments and behavior, I see their heart is not quite as warm and open as they think, in fact, it is more closed than open. In most cases, they are completely closed off from the flow of love.

One of the tendencies of a closed heart is the feeling of being exclusive, superior, or in some way better than other human beings. This closed heart is apparent where there is racism, religious righteousness, or ethnic divisions. I have known many people who will stand up and say, "that is wrong and shameful of those people for having those judgments and feelings of superiority." Yet, in many subtle ways, you might be just as guilty.

For example, do you sneer at the homeless man on the street who asks for money? Do you judge and hold in contempt all those lazy people on welfare feeling that they need to get up and get a job? Do you think because you have a particular college degree or title with a company that you are better than the person who is a labourer?

All of these attitudes are far more subtle but are just as significant forms of closing your heart, shutting yourself off from other people, and shutting yourself off to the flow of love. One of the most common problems I see in people that cut them off from love is arrogance which is nothing more than a form of fear. A way for people to protect themselves from being hurt but, in reality it actually hurts them more in the long run.

People can be arrogant in different ways, such as having an attitude of "I'm more educated than you." There is also religious arrogance, such as "My religion is better than yours." People often have a superficial arrogance, such as "I have more money than you or I have a better job than you or drive a nicer car." All of these are ridiculous ways of closing your heart off and shutting yourself off from the universal flow of love.

This has happened in my own life. For example, after getting my master's degree, I felt that I was somehow better than the other students who didn't have a degree as advanced as mine and especially people who did not have a college degree. It was ridiculous, and to this day I'm embarrassed that I even thought that for a while. These are the sort of things we fall into all the time. Me against the neighbours; me against the Joneses. The comparative, who's got more? All of these tendencies in our thinking shut us off.

They cut us off from other people. Cut us off from our heart, the flow of love, and the goodwill that we need to be connected to our spirit. A person with a truly open heart doesn't look at the covering, doesn't look at the package, but rather, looks at another person's spirit. By virtue of the breath we share, we all have life and because we share that breath, we are all of the same life force.

CHAPTER 4

How an Open Heart Fulfils Your Every Desire

One of the hallmarks of an open heart is that it creates a vibration in you that puts you in resonance with others. Not with their personality or their physical self, but with their spirit. It helps you connect with the authentic self of another person; their spirit. Having an open heart establishes energetic rapport.

An example of having an open heart would be when you walk into a room of people without any judgement. You just love them no matter what they look like or what they are doing, they will feel it. When you do this, an amazing thing will happen, one by one, each person will raise their vibration to meet yours because, essentially, all we ever want is to feel loved.

When your heart is open, it creates synchronicities where you find yourself in the right place at the right time. As your heart begins to open, you start to attract into your life those things that are in exact harmony with what is in your heart. At this point, your heart will help manifest your true desires in life.

You will find that the world begins to organize to meet the strong vibration of an open heart. Life wants to cooperate with you. For example, a person with an open heart will be driving down a busy street where there is no place to park, and then, all of a sudden, someone will pull out of a space right in front of where you want to be. Before you even think about your desire, it manifests.

An open heart releases an exciting kind of energy that makes life fun, but the key is to learn how to love everything you do. Whatever you do, do it with love instead of resentment. It's that simple.

Instead of complaining about your job, love your job. Rather than hating school or a certain class, love going to school and all of your classes

If there is a teacher you don't like, don't be resentful that you have to go to his or her class, rather love the teacher. If the class is difficult for you, love the challenge.

When you meet someone for the first time instead of being judgmental or drawing premature conclusions, just love them. Love them for talking to you instead of someone else.

I have had clients who hated their job because they didn't make enough money or they hated their boss or the long commute. Once they learned to love their job, they actually in some instances doubled their income within a very short time and had other opportunities come their way. This is because of the magnetic and attractive qualities of an open heart.

When your heart opens, life rushes towards you, wanting you to have a happy ending; wanting you to have a fulfilled experience. It feels like there is a conspiracy for your happiness.

There's nothing more attractive and seductive than a person with an open heart. There is a saying, "all the world loves a lover," and it is true. This is what we are all looking for. When you show up and put that loving vibration into the world, all the world will rise to cooperate with you.

Everyone wants to be around the man or woman who is loving their life and living their life with love. This is the power of an open heart, and it's a power that we all possess. It's a right, a gift, and an endowment from the universe. When you open your heart, all that you would ever desire in your heart will move towards you.

CHAPTER 5

The Powerful Healing Lessons of Forgiveness

Forgiveness opens and heals the heart. It brings it back into the wonderful receptive state that it is intended to be in.

It is easy for us to allow our ego to build walls around our injuries and take our wounding from others to epic proportions never allowing us to forgive. If you close your heart and cut yourself off from spirit by focusing on your own wounds, you will suffer.

I have spent many years studying forgiveness and why it is so hard for people to forgive. What I have found is that people have a hidden fear. Most people feel that the injury they incurred, the wounding they felt was deserved.

The problem is that they hide it, and this is really the reason preventing us from moving back into forgiveness.

What you really need to do, to truly move into forgiveness, is to recognize that no one deserves to be treated in an injurious or harmful way. Usually when someone does lash out, they are not even conscious of you, they are just in so much pain and you only happen to be the target.

The key is for you to hold enough self-love and know that you are a magnificent spiritual being. Know that you are lovable and loved. If you know these things then you won't take offense when someone is behaving unkindly. You'll be able to recognize that it's not about you and if it is for some reason, you'll be quicker to say, "I'm sorry, I didn't mean to do that."

If you act like a victim and feel that the world is coming at you in a way that you don't deserve, it will cripple you. It will cause damage to you mentally, physically, and emotionally. It will bring you down and disempower you in a more devastating manner than any other decision you can make. When you forgive, you free yourself of all negative ties to everyone. It really begins with forgiving yourself.

It's alright to make mistakes; we are all spiritual beings having a human experience. When we make a mistake and forgive our self for it, we are calling upon our own divine nature.

We need to look at our mistakes as a learning experience. It's important to remember that we are all doing the best we can at our current level of consciousness. When we are angry and lash out, we are cut off from our spirit; our life force. We are totally in our ego just acting out of fear.

When others injure you, no matter how horrible their acts were, they were simply doing the best they knew how to do at their current level of consciousness. In most cases, their anger really had nothing to do with you.

If you're having trouble forgiving, here are a few questions to ask yourself that can help:

Who are you angry with and what resentments are you holding towards them? How long has it been since you communicated with those who you resent? In what way might you be responsible for the part you played in the separation between you and that person? What decisions can you make that might have been better than the ones you made in the past?

It's alright to be angry but you must understand the function of anger. The function of anger is not to lash out; rather, it is to say, "Stop! No more!" When you are angry, stop and ask yourself what part of you is saying "stop" and what do you want to stop? When you recognize what it is that needs to stop, then anger has served its function.

It's not that we need to get over our anger; rather, we need to embrace it as a messenger. It's telling us that something is out of balance in our life. It could be a judgement, behavior, or some dynamic that needs to come to an end. What can you learn from your anger? Can you, and are you willing to, forgive yourself and those that harmed you to get your life force back?

Look at those people who have caused you pain and injury and ask, what gifts can you find in your interactions with them? What did you learn, gain, or walk away with that has served and benefited you or will help you even by default in your life?

Forgiveness brings life force back into your body and allows all wounds to begin to heal. No injury is worth holding on to because it takes you away from life.

CHAPTER 6

You Are Forgiven – Can You Forgive?

One of the most difficult and often misguided human attributes is to forgive. Forgiveness asks us to look deep within ourselves, and look past hurt, disappointment, and fear. It asks us to look to the deepest corner of our being and seek compassion toward self or others.

Forgiveness is two-fold. A person must be inclined to forgive one's self. An individual who's unable to forgive one's self throughout life's journey, will forever be hounded and weighed down upon. The inability to forgive one's self will hamper the ability to forgive another, for how can one forgive another if they are unwilling or unable to forgive themselves? True forgiveness is born from within, and as such, draws one's gaze toward the individual self, the individual being. As in love, one must be willing to forgive oneself prior to forgiving another.

The second part of forgiveness needs to be approached with true empathy and understanding. Once an individual has been able to successfully forgive themselves, especially for the wrongs they have committed toward themselves in life's journey, then they are able to go outside of themselves and attempt to forgive another or ask for forgiveness from another. Life's most humbling journey is when one can acknowledge a wrong committed against one's-self or another and truly forgive the wrongdoer (be they the individual themselves, another, a community of people, society, or even God).

Forgiveness leads to healing. Forgiveness leads to understanding. Forgiveness leads toward redemption. Forgiveness leads to faith. Forgiveness leads to LOVE. True forgiveness breaks down all barriers and leaves one naked before the other or self. To ask for forgiveness, a person must know what it is like to forgive. To forgive, one must know what it is like to be forgiven.

Forgiveness is a way of life. It brings renewal in times of despair. It brings hope in times of crisis. It brings solitude in times of loneliness. It brings solace in times of hurt. Like LOVE, true forgiveness is not about envy, boasting, or holding qualms. True forgiveness brings understanding and awareness. It's the acknowledgement of some sort of wrongdoing and moving on, moving forward.

Some people and scholars would argue that true forgiveness is a fallacy. Others would argue that in order to achieve *true forgiveness,* one must be willing to forget. I argue that true forgiveness allows us to understand and learn from the wrong done to one's self or another. In order for this to work, forgiveness continually needs to be renewed and rejuvenated. Forgiveness draws its true inspiration from love, and yet, its true goal is love. If we recall the story of the Prodigal Son (Luke 15:11-32):

In the story of the Prodigal Son, we see that the youngest son needed to come to forgive himself first. This forgiveness allows him to come to the awareness that leads him back home. Ultimately, the father is able to forgive the son and take him back in. The eldest son's inability to forgive himself and to continue to live with jealousy toward his brother does not allow him to face the reality of forgiving his brother and the healing power it will bring.

How many times do we look down on ourselves and don't forgive ourselves for our actions and wrong doings? How many times do we dwell upon the moments of life-however insignificant they may seem-and allow them to rob us of our true happiness and love? How many times are we unable to forgive those around us and closest to us for just being themselves? How many times are we unwilling to swallow our own pride and ask for forgiveness, especially when we know we're in the wrong?

The inability to forgive ourselves and others, and ask for forgiveness from ourselves and others robs us of our passions, loves, joys, and time. This inability leaves us with doubt, fear, regret failure and disappointment. To forgive is Divine. Forgiveness helps us to transcend the physical realm and move into the spiritual realm.

Forgiveness brings us ever closer to God. It is one of the few human actions that help us to heal physical, emotional, and psychological hurts. Since it's an action that requires both internal and external actions, it forces us into another realm. To forgive is not a natural human act, but one that, if born from the right spark, can bring much healing in all the areas of our lives.

Forgive thoroughly:

If someone is always speaking condemnation to you, you must realize two things. First, the resentment, bitterness, and anger that caused them to become this way is neither your possession nor your obligation. Second, you're not obligated to stay in their presence or be in their company. Don't adopt their hate or assimilate their pain.

Forgiveness power:

You and I have the power to forgive and to be forgiven. Ask for forgiveness from those whom you feel you have wronged. When you ask for their forgiveness, you should be determined in your heart that you will do your best to be better next time, knowing that sometimes your best isn't good enough.

Asking for their forgiveness doesn't automatically imply that they'll forgive you, so you must accept the outcome; again knowing you have done all you can do. The law is now at work in them as it is in you; they must forgive you if they wish to be forgiven.

"Therefore, if you are offering your gift at the altar and then remember that your brother or sister has something against you; leave your gift there in front of the altar. First go and be reconciled to that person; then come and offer your gift." Matthew 5:23

Be only the best you can be. We are ever striving to be the best we can be. Don't strive to become someone else, or to meet someone else's unrealistic expectations based on their own greed or ambition. Learn to be happy with the best that you are. Don't judge yourself too harshly and learn to forgive yourself and others quickly. Release yourself from the perceived obligations of guilt; focus on the positive aspects of relationship. Always be sure that the speck of dust you see in your neighbour's eye isn't really the plank you have in your own eye.

You can't create in someone else's reality. Ask no one to be different so that you can feel good. Release yourself from the weight of responsibility of needing to control the world. If you do, you will be happy in life because the crack in the sidewalk is just a crack, no one is to blame. It doesn't need to be fixed. We just need to learn to lift our feet a bit higher.

Anthony Robbins coined a word: CANI! It means Constant and Never-ending Improvement. In short it describes the process of consciously finding something every day to improve.

Once your truth is found, then set your goals based on your truth. This is the truth; our Father in heaven is the one true God. He is all things to us. He forgave us. So, likewise we must forgive. By holding pain, hurt, and transgression against others we only hurt ourselves.

Forgiveness is the beginning of spiritual health.

Make goals you can accomplish. The accomplishment thereof will reinforce your faith. Faith is the substance of the things you hope for and will provide you with a complete and abundant life.

Martin Luther King once said, "The supreme act of courage is that of forgiving ourselves. That which I was not but could have been. That which I would have done but did not do. Can I find the fortitude to remember in truth, to understand, to submit, to forgive, and to be free to move on in time?"

I had a client who broke his neck. He was taken into surgery and through the marvels of modern medicine was able to regain an active life. However, his neck never stopped hurting and the range of motion he had with his head was limited. Usually his pain wasn't severe and he adjusted to the inability to look straight up. After a few years, he told me, "I am as healed as I'm going to be, but I'm daily aware of my neck."

Sometimes, forgiveness is like this. You're as healed as you're going to get but you still have the scars and sometimes they hurt. They shouldn't keep you from moving forward.

Jesus was tempted in every way we are tempted today. The difference between Jesus and us is that Jesus did not sin. He understands when we do sin. He understands what we are going through. The Apostle Paul tells us in Hebrews that when we as Christians do sin, we can go boldly before the throne of God and ask and receive forgiveness. How wonderful God the Father is, when we do sinful things, He forgives us.

We may profess Jesus as our Saviour, but not live as if Jesus is the Lord of our lives. Look at your life, there are so many areas we miss God's direction. Are you an alcoholic, do you use drugs, do you have a terrible temper and abuse

your loved ones, are you neglectful of your children or your parents? It doesn't matter - all that matters is knowing God loves us all equally.

In Romans 2:11 it says that "there is no respect of persons with God" I take this to mean that God does not play favourites. He loves your worst enemy as much as he loves you. We are all born with free will. There are lessons in each lifetime we must learn in order for our soul to grow and reunite with our spirit. We have the free will to determine when we will learn those lessons but not if we will learn them.

"And forgive us our sins, just as we have forgiven those who have sinned against us."Matthew 6:12

The King James says, "our debts" for the term "our sins."

We are to forgive others just as we have been forgiven. Have you ever really thought about that? We are to forgive others with God's forgiveness. We are to forgive others just like God forgives us!

"Your heavenly Father will forgive you if you forgive those who sin against you; but if you refuse to forgive them, he will not forgive you." Matthew 6:14

God forgives us as we forgive others. That is so awe inspiring! God forgives us but He expects us to forgive others, and then He forgives us as we forgive others!

CHAPTER 7

The Incredible Healing Power of Laughter

Whenever we feel out of sync, victimized, or things in our life are out of control we either withdraw from life or we amplify it by becoming bullies. One of the best ways to disengage from the illusion of feeling powerless is laughter.

Laughter snaps you out of the illusion of feeling powerless and puts you into what I call the witness position where you are no longer in the subjective and vulnerable mode. You start to look at yourself as detached.

If you can laugh at something, you won't be victimized by it. Begin to look at all of life with a sense of humor. Laughter is power. When you are afraid of something, laugh. It gives you a sense of perspective. When you laugh, the world laughs with you.

Laugh at yourself. Laugh at everything. Always remember, a situation may be critical, but it's never serious. In order to have a happy and fulfilling life you need to learn how to play the fool. Be the first to laugh at yourself and look at the seriousness of your own vulnerabilities.

I teach my clients and the people who attend my workshops that whenever you're experiencing drama, go look in the mirror because what you're are looking at looks pretty silly. The more wretched and intense your face looks, the more laughable it is.

Actively give yourself doses of humor every day whether it's a funny show on television or a movie, you need to make it a habit. When you move into laughter, it's a great way to take in oxygen and breath is power. Laughter is an amplifier of the breath. It turns the oxygen in your lungs completely over and gives you a fresh blood supply.

The harder you laugh the more oxygen you have in your lungs. Laughter releases endorphins that have great healing power. There are many studies that show how empowering laughter is. If you're feeling weak, vulnerable and out of control laughter is a good way to bring yourself back into balance?

A funny movie, a silly book, a good joke, and the ability to look at your own situation with a sense of humor will restore you back to balance very quickly.

One of the biggest benefits of a good laugh is that when we start laughing at a situation and seeing the silliness or the humor or the ridiculousness of our own human drama, it reminds us instantly that there is a power greater than we are recognizing.

It is this greater power that tells us that there is something bigger than all of us in the universe that is your highest form of balancing your life. By surrendering your own personal will over to God's will, you are actually taking your own power back.

The truth is, something put that breath of life in you, something greater than you could ever control or imagine is keeping your heart beating. Something greater than you is behind the order and design of the entire universe and that power deemed you worthy to exist.

This greater power deemed you worthy to breathe and to be on earth. It is looking after you with incredible love and compassion, with care better than you could ever manufacture on your own.

CHAPTER 8

Unleashing Your Inner Power through Deep Breathing

One of the most common problems I run into with people is that they are afraid. I have seen this in all type of venues. For example, people are afraid when they go to social engagements. They are afraid of meeting and interacting with people they have never met before.

People are often afraid when they go shopping. They're afraid they are going to be taken advantage of or they might buy the wrong thing. Many people are afraid to drive. They are afraid of other drivers and getting into an accident.

When you become afraid you stop breathing. Breath is power and when you hold your breath you lose that power. When you breathe, your center of power and boundaries get bigger and bigger. You set the intention of being safe, "no one is going to mess with me." There is power in your breath.

One of the biggest problems people have is that their breathing is very shallow. So often when people have a lot of anxiety, they reach for prescription drugs and alcohol to curb their feelings. These don't improve your life at all, they only make things worse.

Breath is spirit, when you breathe in deeply through the nose, you are bringing the power of your spirit into your body, and when you exhale through your mouth, you are getting rid of all the anxiety and fear inside of you.

When you first wake up in the morning, take at least ten deep breathes to start your day. When you feel anger or anxiety coming on during the day, stop and take three deep breaths before you react or say anything. You will feel a calming because spirit is in your body.

When you practice deep breathing and create a pure vibration of intention, you are invincible. If you can create such a clear sense of what is true for you and put your full power of decision behind that, no one will mess with you. It is an awesome power. So awesome that nothing can stop you.

My favourite example of this is the story of Mahatma Gandhi who liberated India by pure intention and not a single gun was raised. He just decided, "It's time to be free." It was the bloodless revolution of India.

Intention and decision, if pure, are invincible. The important thing about getting to that place is to get really clear and really specific about what's true for you. What is your limit? That kind of intention, that kind of courage to face down violation and someone's intrusion into your space is power.

If you have the ability to say "no" without any reservation, people will not even test you. They won't even go there. Someone who really knows their boundaries is also extraordinarily respectful of other people's boundaries. When this is the case, everyone feels mutually benefitted and safe.

When you know what works for you and you're really honest about it, you will not ask someone else to violate their boundaries. It just would not be consistent with who you really are.

Boundaries and sovereignty are about taking honest responsibility and control over your life. Doing, to the best of your ability, what really is correct for you, no more and no less?

CHAPTER 9

Healing Physical and Emotional Problems with Spiritual Power – Mind Body Healing

One of the greatest opportunities you have in your life is to get in touch with your higher self for healing. You can transform challenging emotions, physical ailments, difficulties, and negative thinking by making the connection with a part of yourself that is already whole and complete. Meditation and prayer can help you to maintain this awareness. You just need to have the intention to make contact with the healing power within you, and as you ask, it answers.

Here are a few techniques you can use to help you:

- You can ask questions of your higher power, such as, "Is there any assistance I can have from my spiritual self? If so, how can I best be in touch with it?"

- You may want to ask for the assistance and support of a spiritual being, such as Jesus, the Divine Mother, Buddha, Moses, Mohammed, or any other great spiritual inspiration. You might experience this support in the form of healing light, higher wisdom and guidance, love, and healing power.

- Healing guides may come to assist. They have also been called "Divine Doctors" or "Inner Healers." You might want to go within and experience yourself climbing up five stairs into a special inner room. There you can meet special healing guides who will make specific physical adjustments to your body and mind. Such as removing headaches, altering tumors, smoothing out tense muscles. The possibilities are infinite.

- You can ask for healing Light to come in various forms as you go within.

Here are a few of them:

- · A laser which shines on a specific ailment or issue.

- · Streaming beams (like sunbeams) from the universe, bringing light to whatever your problem might be.

- · Beams from within the heart center, coming forth from within you to heal.

- · A whirling golden ball that begins at the top of the head and proceeds downward, cleansing all the chakras or energy centers.

- · A healing room full of light beams radiating from walls, floors, and ceiling.

- · A ray from the palm of your hand which you can apply to any pain or difficulty.

- · Any other ideas you may have

- You can work with healing water. Because water is a great cleanser and preserver, it is ideal to use in mind body healing. You can go within a pond of healing water or a waterfall, water that is the perfect temperature and depth. The water brings relaxation and relief, and it washes away all difficulty, all pain, physical and emotional. After this, you can imagine coming out of the water into the radiant healing rays of the sun. The water can also wash over your physical body like a waterfall, cleansing away discomfort of any kind.

- You may be able to handle pain and illness more easily by experiencing spiritual comfort through a transformed perspective. You may be able to understand the problems of your life in expanded ways, including having greater faith in the direction you're going and where you've been, acceptance of whatever you need to handle as a process of learning, finding meaning and growth opportunities in illness, learning compassion, understanding the role of prayer in the healing process, and finding a way to transcend the experience of the body.

One of the greatest powers you have is to have the knowledge of how to work in alignment with your higher consciousness to heal your body and mind. It's a wonderful gift that you've been given.

CHAPTER 10

Strengthening Your Personal Sovereignty by Setting Boundaries

Boundaries are part of your personal motivation. They tell the world how much responsibility you want to carry forward in keeping your life true to what it is that you really care about. It is the center of decisions, choice, and ethics. They represent integrity and responsibility for your own life experience.

If your power of decision aligns with your highest good, then your experience in life will reflect that. If you give away your power by not taking responsibility and feeling that you have no choice, then your life experience will reflect this as well. Your life will be oppressed, overwhelmed, and taken away from you.

You can either seize your power by being the sovereign King or Queen of your own life where you have integrity and are in alignment with your truth, or just be one of the subjects in someone else's kingdom.

Strong boundaries help you govern your day to day experiences. Do you govern them with a sense of authority? Do you govern them with a sense of personal power?

When you have strong personal boundaries, you will feel strong. You will be able to make decisions that truly support you and stick with them. You will think before you act and you will say things that only reflect your truth.

Personal boundaries make you a very powerful person because people know how far they can go with you. Boundaries allow you to set up what does and doesn't work for you. They give a sense of "don't mess with me, don't challenge me, and don't take advantage of me." You are very confident and it gives others a sense that you are fully present.

Without strong boundaries, you will be weak. You will be a victim and blame others for your experiences. "It's not my fault. He or she is doing it to me. I'm oppressed." You'll feel incapable, give up easily, and resign yourself to what you don't want.

A clear hallmark of a person without boundaries is they are a long suffering martyr. A person who gives and gives and feels as though no one is giving back; a person who says "yes" all the time and doesn't know how to say no and ask for what they want.

People with strong boundaries aren't afraid of saying "this works for me and that doesn't." The stronger your boundaries are, the more you make it safe for others. If you clearly know your boundaries, then those around you will also begin to feel safe.

An example of a person without boundaries is the over indulgent parent who gives in to every single whim and whine of their demanding child. The more they give, the more their child asks for, and the more their child asks for, the more they give until ultimately the parent feels pushed around and out of control.

At this point, both the parent and the child feel unsafe because there is a feeling that no one is in charge. There are no clearly defined boundaries that this is acceptable and this is not. It only corrects itself when the parent puts his or her foot down that enough is enough.

Setting boundaries is hard for many people to do. You have to decide, "this works for me and this doesn't." You have to know when to say yes and when to say no, and most importantly, you have a right to express yourself in every situation.

If each person has their own clear sense of boundaries then peace will prevail. It's when the boundaries are not clear, "what is mine, what is yours, how far can I go, how far can't I go?" This is where conflict erupts.

When you have solid boundaries, you become the peacekeeper because the more clear you are about what works for you, the more tolerant and interesting you become in what works for others. The power struggle then ceases.

A person with strong personal boundaries is a safe person to be around because they clearly know the truth for themselves and the decisions they make are right. This allows everyone to be at peace.

The Transformational Power of Blessing

As I have said throughout this book, the greatest need we have as human beings is to love and to be loved. Our capacity to love is directly related to being able to open up our heart at its deepest level. We spend most of our lives closed off to other people's suffering.

We tend to give lip service to others' suffering by saying how terrible it is that the person is having to go through this situation. It makes us temporarily feel good that we have at least acknowledged it and then we get back to our lives. It is as if we are afraid that if we get to close we will somehow get drawn into another person's suffering.

Opening ourselves up to other people's suffering is called compassion. This is difficult for most people to do because of the nature of our world. We live the majority of our lives in our ego which is based on fear. We don't want to open up and show true heartfelt compassion to others for fear that we will be hurt.

In order to show true compassion for others, you must transform from your ego - based life to a spirit guided life. One of the best ways I have found to connect with your spirit and live from that highest frequency is by learning to bless everyone. When you bless another person it opens up a path to eventually being able to love everyone unconditionally.

There are particular techniques for blessing others that are very powerful. Most religions have standard formulas for blessing people. My two favourite blessings come from the Christian and Tibetan traditions. In the Christian tradition, the blessing is, "May the peace of God which passeth all understanding be with you now and forever."

There are certain words in this blessing that I find very powerful: "which passeth all understanding." I believe this means that which transcends the intellect, that which is beyond our judgment. "Peace of God", is the silence of the ocean of being which is always there beyond our understanding, beyond our thoughts. May everyone have this peace? How can anyone ever argue with that? How can we not wish that for everyone? Whether it is for someone we consider a friend or an enemy?

In the Tibetan tradition the blessing is, "Om manipadme hum." In this wonderful blessing "Om" invokes the infinite, enlightenment, fulfilment; it is the jewel we are always searching for at any moment in our life.

"Padme" means lotus, that which spreads everywhere and is found everywhere including in our own heart.

Most people wish other people the best, so let's say for example you notice a homeless person on a street corner. Instead of looking at him or her through the prism of your intellect and having disgust as to why the person can't just get a job and make a positive contribution to society, bless them instead.

You could wish him or her to find a job, better judgment, good health, to find a home and have a better life. This tries to encompass too much for the person because you can continually find more and more wishes for the person and it never ends. Instead, it's better to silently bless the person. By blessing the person, you are wishing him or her the jewel of existence, which is found everywhere including in ourselves.

The way I bless people and advise my clients is to just walk through crowds such as when you are in a mall, a movie theatre, or even the DMV and silently or quietly under your breath say either the Christian or Tibetan blessings. When we bless another person, we witness their true self, their spirit.

There has always been much disagreement over the ages between spiritual masters and teachers as to whether or not blessing another person actually helps them, but what they all agree on is that it does something very powerful for us when we do it.

Blessing other people pokes holes in the hard outer shell of our ego and shatters it. It moves us out of our intellect where we have the false belief that somehow we are better than someone else because of the amount of money we make or a certain title or position we may have. It liberates us and moves us into the identity of our spirit.

Rather than going through life moment to moment, trying to keep everyone else's suffering at arm's length. Blessing another person invites compassion in. It opens our heart to the suffering of others and in the process, we discover that it doesn't hurt us. Our heart is big enough to transform it.

The English Poet, William Blake wrote, "Love to faults is always blind, always is to joy inclined. Lawless, winged, and unconfined, and breaks all chains from every mind."

Whatever type of blessing resonates for you to bestow on others, it will expand your heart and your ability to love unconditionally. We don't have to be told to love one another we should just do. Love can't be forced. It has to grow in our lives. This is the transformational power of blessing.

CHAPTER 11

Bringing It All Together

In today's current political climate where we appear to be so divided, there are many groups of people who want different interests and want change, but it cannot happen without changing yourself first. Protests and fighting are not going to do the job for us. This is all out of fear of loving our self; we don't want to do it because it's scary and hard.

This is difficult, and most people don't want to do it. They would rather try to impose their will on other people and make them change. This will never bring about peace and harmony; it will only cause more difficulty and chaos.

We are part of an all loving benevolent universe that doesn't play favorites. God loves us all equally. Everything in the universe is energy in motion so we attract into our lives what we put out. If we put out anger, chaos and negativity that is what we will attract back into our lives. On the other hand, if we put out peace and unconditional self-love then we will attract peace and love into our lives.

Philosopher and inspirational author Dr. Wayne Dyer said, "We don't attract into our lives what we want, we attract what we are."

In order to make fundamental change bringing about peace and harmony in the world, you have to take the journey inward and work on yourself first. So many people claim that they want to reach out and change the county, and in some cases the world, but you can't do it unless you first change yourself. That starts with learning to love yourself unconditionally. You have to learn to love yourself before you can truly love another person. You have to learn to love yourself before you can really reach out with genuine love and help another person.

Change starts with each individual person. We are all an extension of God; Beautiful divine beings. No one is here by accident, we incarnated into this physical form for a purpose. This purpose is to co-create with the universe. To learn, enjoy life, and make this world a better place because we were here. We are all part of the interwoven netting of the universe, all equally important to the whole.

We live in a capitalist society that often conditions us to believe that there are winners and losers. Where we are judged by the title we have in a company or how much money we have, or even by the type of car we drive.

This physical life of ours will end at some point, people don't like to face that, and our ego doesn't because it dies with our physical body, but our soul and spirit live on for infinity. When we allow making more and more money to be the main purpose in life, we become disconnected from God. It forces us to live in our ego and there is no greater amputation that we can suffer on the physical plane than being disconnected from our spirit.

Our ego is constantly trying to convince us of how great we are because of how much money we make, or the position in business, or the title in politics we have and that is all out of fear. It is not our true and authentic self.

Our intellect is simply our physical life which will end at some point. Most people don't want to face that. Our ego doesn't because it dies with our physical body but our soul and spirit life on for infinity. I'm not saying that capitalism is bad. In fact, capitalism has helped millions of people make a living and support their family. It has raised the standard of living for millions of people all over the world. We just cannot forget who we really are; spiritual beings having a human experience. We have to stop taking life so seriously and understand our purpose; to love, enjoy our life on the physical plane, and co-create with the Universe. When we take life too seriously we miss so much of all the enjoyment and fulfillment it has to offer. St. Francis of Assisi said, "Wear the world as a loose garment which touches us in a few places and there lightly."

In the book of Romans 12:2 it says "Do not be conformed to this world, but be transformed by the renewal of your mind, that by testing you may discern what is the will of God, what is good and acceptable and perfect" In John 17:16 Jesus said "They are not of the world, just as I am not of the world. As believers, we should be set apart from this world."

I believe all of these quotes to mean that so many people are too invested in their own ego, their own needs and their own perceptions of themselves that they have forgotten not only who they really are but the most important need we have in life. To love and be loved.

We incarnate to learn the lessons we need to learn in this life in order for our soul to grow and reconnect with our spirit and ultimately become one with God. In learning these lessons we are not only helping our own soul growth but everyone else's around us because we are all part of the whole, equally important.

Learning our lessons for soul growth is not an option. We will all come full circle and learn what we need to grow either in this lifetime or the next. It is up to our own individual free will that God gives us as to when we will learn these lessons, but not if.

When you learn to stop judging, love yourself, and in turn love everyone else unconditionally, then you will be able to manifest whatever your heart desires and you will truly be able to have a magical life.

May the Divine Spirit bless you always on your journey.

Joe Love.

RESOURCES

Free Newsletter

Would you like to receive informative articles that can help you connect with your spirit and reach advanced states of consciousness? Sign up for my email newsletter. It's free and packed with practical tools and techniques you can use to develop your intuitive abilities and then use this natural gift to expand your awareness and reconnect with your higher self. In addition, this monthly newsletter provides strategies for living a happier, more fulfilling, and balanced life.

To sign up for my newsletter got to: **www.joeloveiw.com**

Consultations

I will guide and mentor you through a personal consultation. In our time spent together, I will reveal your soul plan, your soul's purpose, your soul lessons, and address obstacles that you are currently facing. Then we will look at where you are today and how you can best align with your life's plan, overcome your blocks and get into the grace and flow immediately.

The result is a quick solution and a return to the peace that you want and deserve. Once you are shown how to align with your soul plan, you will be relieved of stress, wasted time, and fear so you will be able to return to your most authentic spirit and be able to live as you want. To Schedule a 30 or 60 minute reading go to **www.joeloveiw.com or call 866-212—0608**

Seminars and Workshops

I will conduct a half or full day workshop on the subjects of sixth sensory living, working with your spirit guides, manifesting your desires, chakra balancing, mind/body health, and creating extraordinary relationships.

My seminars and workshops can also be customized to fit your individual needs.

For more information about my workshops and seminars go to **www.joeloveiw.com or call 866-212-0608**

www.ingramcontent.com/pod-product-compliance
Lightning Source LLC
Chambersburg PA
CBHW041358090426
42741CB00001B/4